Mountain Men

RACHEL GOODCHILD

PHOTOGRAPHY BY JOHN BOUGEN

PENGUIN BOOKS

PENGUIN BOOKS

Published by the Penguin Group

Penguin Group (NZ), 67 Apollo Drive, Rosedale,
North Shore 0632, New Zealand (a division of Pearson New Zealand Ltd)
Penguin Group (USA) Inc., 375 Hudson Street,
New York, New York 10014, USA
Penguin Group (Canada), 90 Eglinton Avenue East, Suite 700, Toronto,
Ontario, M4P 2Y3, Canada (a division of Pearson Penguin Canada Inc.)
Penguin Books Ltd, 80 Strand, London, WC2R 0RL, England
Penguin Ireland, 25 St Stephen's Green,
Dublin 2, Ireland (a division of Penguin Books Ltd)
Penguin Group (Australia), 250 Camberwell Road, Camberwell,
Victoria 3124, Australia (a division of Pearson Australia Group Pty Ltd)
Penguin Books India Pvt Ltd, 11, Community Centre,
Panchsheel Park, New Delhi – 110 017, India
Penguin Books (South Africa) (Pty) Ltd, 24 Sturdee Avenue,
Rosebank, Johannesburg 2196, South Africa

Penguin Books Ltd, Registered Offices: 80 Strand, London, WC2R 0RL, England

First published by Penguin Group (NZ), 2008
1 3 5 7 9 10 8 6 4 2

Copyright © Rachel Goodchild, 2008

The right of Rachel Goodchild to be identified as the author of this work in terms of
section 96 of the Copyright Act 1994 is hereby asserted.

Designed by Alice Bell
Prepress by Image Centre Ltd
Printed in China through Bookbuilders, Hong Kong

ISBN: 9780143007517

A catalogue record for this book is available from the National Library of New Zealand.

www.penguin.co.nz

Contents

Avoca, near Lake Pearson.

Introduction

TACITURN, STOIC AND MEN OF PURE UNDERSTATEMENT, these men of the high country are completely tied to the beauty and the strength of their surroundings.

Each one came to the hills for different reasons and while some have moved away, they all speak of the fondness they hold for the expanse of sky, the places of peaceful reflection and the social times they had on the job or together at the end of a hard day's work.

Some have seen huge changes, their family land sold and lost to future generations or are struggling to decide who might carry the farm on. Others have worked on or around the land, never owning it, but love it just as deeply.

It is hard not to be taken in by each man's devotion to his land, his horse, his dog. There is something raw and strong about it, something that is so very far removed from modern urban living. There is a connection these men have to the rhythm of the seasons, the changes of their environment that is quite foreign to the great many of us.

Each man in this book trusts that the land will remain connected to them for the remainder of their life. More than one of them mentioned their desire to live out in the hills till their very last breath, with only the craggy rocks marking their resting place.

These men of the high country love being men. They feel comfortable in their maleness, enjoy traditionally male pursuits and build strong deep friendships with other men. There were no apologies for being a bloke as I interviewed each one—nor should there be. They are who they are: men of the mountain. Nothing more, nothing less.

Paddy Freaney

ARTHUR'S PASS, PUB OWNER AND

MOUNTAIN EXPLORER

Paddy came out from the UK en route from
Australia and heading out to South America.
He never quite made it to South America and instead
settled—as much as an adventure-seeking, ex-SAS
man can settle—in Arthur's Pass in the South Island.

Waimakariri River,
near Bealey Spur.

I HAVE BEEN LIVING UP AT ARTHUR'S PASS since 1969. I came to New Zealand as part of a planned round-the-world trip with my Land Rover—I would ship it from country to country and tour around discovering little pockets here and there. I was halfway around by the time I got here, and never quite managed to leave.

I was in the SAS in Britain before they got famous. I got to see many out-of-the-way places and have been all throughout the Middle East. We got to do some great jobs but it was all on the quiet. The SAS never hit the news really until after I was gone.

I stay in touch with all my SAS mates—there is a lot of networking that goes on between us guys. There are plenty of reunions and I write a bit for their magazine off and on. Each of the team has ended up scattered all over the globe.

I bought a house up here in 1971 and spent a bit of time working in jobs and a few businesses in Christchurch. I bought a bit of land up here in 1980 and put the Bealey Hotel up on it. People thought I was mad. They thought a hotel and pub wouldn't work up here. They were wrong. I built it and while I no longer run it, I am still its owner and am there most days. I have sold a lease on it, which allows me to now do what I want with my life and enjoy my days.

I also set up an outdoor education centre in Arthur's Pass that was very popular. I sold it later to the Canterbury Education Board. I have always enjoyed being outdoors, and in particular climbing. It was during a recreational climb out here with a friend that I spotted the moa.

It is all very well documented. Many people think it is just a myth but I know what we saw that day. A friend of mine was getting over an operation and we went out for a long walk. We thought we might do a bit of shooting so we took a rifle out with us as well. My partner Michelle came for the journey. We were all looking forward to a good day out.

We had been out walking for about four hours. I was up ahead a bit further. I saw this huge dark bird in the bush in front of me. At first I just stood and stared but then I realised I had to get the others to see it so I rushed back and brought them back up to where I had seen it. One of the guys had a camera and got a photo of it.

I know some people think it is all a bit of a laugh but ask any one of us and I can tell you we will each swear black and blue that we saw it. We are convinced to this day. We were all invited by the New Zealand Skeptics to tell them about our experience. We were up on the stage for three hours fielding questions, getting completely grilled. By the end of the evening they were all so impressed with our ability to stick to our story that they shouted us beers for the rest of the evening!

Since then I have taken in quite a few groups of people to see if they could find it again. I have some good friends, including a doctor friend from Otago and another guy who is the

I had a Japanese film crew come in with me to try and find the moa. And doubters are always coming in to the pub to argue with me. If they ask for me I just tell them I'm out—and that they are talking to my brother!

president of the New Zealand Skeptics, come out with me every now and again. The 'doc' is even studying the possibility of moa still being around. A few seasons back he found some fresh chompings in trees right at moa height. I know some people will never believe but we all know there are moa out there somewhere.

I take people in by helicopter too. I had a Japanese film crew come in with me to try and find the moa. And, of course, doubters are always coming in to the pub to argue with me. If they ask for me I normally just tell them I'm out—and that they are talking to my brother!

I had a great moa shipped over from the West Coast to sit outside my pub. It is a huge thing—it weighs two and a half tonnes. It has some similar-looking companions at a café and tearooms near Alfred Forest. I used to go down and ask them if I could buy them for my hotel, as I thought they looked perfect. Every time I asked, the answer would be the same. They were not for sale.

Out of the blue one day, this woman calls me up on the phone. She had a great name: Joy Heaven. (Not a religious woman, though!) She owned the tearooms and told me the moa were for sale. I asked her if they could be delivered and she said that wouldn't be part of the deal. I wasn't sure if I really wanted to own them any longer but was pretty tempted as they were so beautiful. I decided I had to go and get them.

Of course, trying to find a way of getting

them back to the Bealey was a bit tricky. I rang my mate 'Bones' and asked if he could help. I said we need to shift some moa. He asked how many and I said just two. He was OK with that, so we arranged to go and collect them.

We went down to Alfred Forest and loaded them on to the truck. They were very heavy—we didn't need to weigh them down. They nodded their heads to everyone as we drove them back on the way home. It wasn't too long a trip; it takes around an hour and a half most days to get back from there.

That's on a normal day, however. With two moa in the back, it was obviously anything but a 'normal' day. We noticed the petrol was looking a little low so thought we should make a brief detour to fill up. We somehow found ourselves outside a pub and thought it might be a good idea to have a wee drink. People loved the moa. They came and took their photos with them.

The trip was a laugh a minute. We decided it wasn't fair to stop at just the one pub. So we stopped at all of those on the way home, which slowed us down a bit—our normal one-and-half-hour trip took 10 hours! We didn't get home until 10 p.m. that night! What a great day. Come to think of it, I don't think we ever got the petrol topped up.

I'm so glad we went and got them, as they have been worth their weight in gold. They really add to the Bealey and look great.

I have always enjoyed climbing. I like to get out and climb the peaks around here—it has always been a passion of mine. I like the fact that you can just pull on your boots and get out on to a mountain for a climb.

Of course, there are times when the body suffers. We do party a bit out here and I can feel a bit worse for wear as a result sometimes. But then I go out and flog the body to death, which keeps me alive. It can be a bit risky but it is always worth it. There is the risk of getting caught out in the snow too. I've had times when I've been trapped in the huts for days but you take it as a chance to let your body recover before you get going again.

In 1976 I spent the summer climbing every mountain in New Zealand, all 31 of them. I got to train as a mountain guide in the first ever guide course held in New Zealand and though I have never practised as a guide the experience was invaluable.

Because I was well known for my climbing, I have been able to go to some amazing places. I went to Antarctica one summer, which was fantastic. That was an experience to remember. With my outdoor interest and experience I was able to get in on a team going there. It was a great place to drink, I can tell you.

We went on a tour around Ireland last year, which I named the 'peaks and pubs tour'. This year we plan to climb the mountains in Africa. Next week I am taking a fella from Brazil out to climb Mount Murchison. He is not very fit, unlike me, so it might be a bit hard going for him.

This morning I went and put my three grandsons on a plane back to the UK. We had

I like to get out and climb the peaks around here—it has always been a passion of mine. I like the fact that you can just pull on your boots and get out on to a mountain for a climb.

them here for a month and we did it all: jet boating, caving, the luge, abseiling, diving, parasailing, walking on the glaciers, bungy-jumping and almost every other activity you can think of. They will have slept well on the trip back!

There is so much around us to do that is interesting to visitors. Entertaining them all does mean I have less time for climbing and I am again beginning to feel the need to get out there for another expedition.

I am a believer in juggling things and putting your life on the line. I can safely look at my life and feel there has never been a dull moment. It is a matter of balancing what you want to do with what you can do but also pushing your personal limits all the time.

I have never been a farmer out here, but being surrounded by farms means I know a lot about sheep. I have helped out when local farmers have needed a hand with all manner of things from tailing to docking to drenching. Sometimes I've thought it would be nice to have a farm, even if only to ride around on a horse, enjoying the wide open spaces.

I am now at the point where I want to enjoy my life. My past businesses were very successful and I don't need to do that again. I am a canny investor and can generally manage without having to start something fresh. I turn down a lot of good ideas. There is always someone somewhere wanting me to invest my time and money into something new. But I've spent years going after ideas and building things. The old hotel, for example, was a nutty idea that was very successful. I often see bargain properties and know I could make money on them but I just tell myself I don't need it and to keep away.

I spent my life trying to make something, and my money was always blown on a new expedition. Now it is time to enjoy living here at Arthur's Pass. We have a permanent population of around 52, with a pile of what we call transients who come and go. Some of them love it as much as we do and become permanents along with us. This is definitely the place for me. I became a Kiwi after I got an official letter from the government asking me to make it all proper. I got a local Justice of the Peace to sign my pass—I didn't even need to leave Arthur's Pass to do it. People ask me if I will ever go back home to the UK. I just tell them I am still saving up.

Roger Mason

Darfield, musterer, farmer and contractor

The moment Roger crossed the river to Mt Algidus
Station, he felt like he had left childhood behind and
become a man. The days on the station shaped him,
leading him to spend his working adult life in the
high country, on the hills and farms.

Methven Rodeo.

I ARRIVED AT MT ALGIDUS STATION EIGHT days shy of my 16th birthday. Growing up, all I had ever wanted to be was a carpenter, but just before I was due to start my apprenticeship, the two brothers I was going to serve my time with split the partnership up and didn't want to take on anyone new.

I had read a book on the high country and thought that way of life sounded exciting. My step-dad knew Ron Anderson whose wife Mona was a well-known high-country author. He said he would talk to them both about taking me on at Mt Algidus. He told me to look out for their blue Holden when it arrived next door at Mona's parents' place so he could go down to ask Ron about getting a job for me.

It wasn't too long before I saw the blue car there and I went home and told my step-dad right away. He went and had a chat and I got a job. A month later I had packed my swag and was off.

We had to cross the river to get there. The station owned some big old army trucks that were high off the ground and used to cross over. I came to high-country farming just as they were starting to swap over from the old ways to the new—the wagon and horses had only stopped being used about two months before I got there.

When the river was up we would be stranded at the station for up to two weeks. We would not be able to get our mail or bread or anything. It was about a 15-mile trip to get the mail and the only way was across the river.

I never really realised at the time, but looking back I realise I did a lot of river work. If Mona was away and the river was high, it was up to me to find a way over to pick her up. If we needed to cross with the truck, it was me who would be sent out to find a good ford for crossing.

We always had about five station hacks that we used for river crossings. They were stabled in the evening to be covered and fed chaff, and then turned out for the night. We would stable them again in the morning and feed them once more.

Upon arriving at the Wilberforce River, we would chaff into sacks to feed the hacks still working down at the station. I'd throw my swag on top and ride with it up high on the chaff across the river to my new home. I got on that truck a boy and by the time I crossed the river, I was a man.

I came to high-country farming just as they were starting to swap over from the old ways to the new—the wagon and horses had only stopped being used about two months before I got there.

We had a gang of regular staff there in those days. There was the station cook, a cowman gardener who milked the house cows and tended the gardens, the head shepherd and another shepherd. We had seasonal musterers who helped from August to May, too. It was a large station to cover—about 100,000 acres.

I was there for six years, give or take a season. I worked on a nearby station. I actually worked there during the same time that Mona Anderson wrote her books on the high country. She was a lovely lady. She'd often cook for us down at the homestead if the station cook wasn't around.

In many ways it was a man-only zone up there—with Mona the only woman. She was great, though; she treated us as if we were her boys. She was a real mum figure to us. I was such a young fella there and she really looked after me. I had a real problem with boils at one stage and she made many poultices to draw the core out.

I remember she took it upon herself to teach some of the men how to dance. I already knew, but these chaps were very proud with themselves that they could manage a few steps. She convinced them that it would be fun to go to a dance in Methven after the autumn muster. We all went down there for the evening. Seems they were a little less confident when they had to test their skills out for real and spent much of the night watching everyone else dance. It was a little too scary for them.

The high-country life can make you a little shy sometimes. It tangles you up in your own little world and you can stop feeling part of anything else but what is out under the sky.

I remember a particularly shy guy who came and visited us when were at Algidus; it was one of the deer cullers who came in for some supplies and more ammunition. He was one of their best cullers. The government contracted them and he had to collect the tails to prove he had killed them all. Well, he was so shy. I think it took about two hours for him to make eye contact with anyone. He had been back country for so long that he could barely remember how to talk to another person.

I remember trying to talk to him—Gerald Goodger was his name—and he was just so quiet. He wasn't a wimp or anything, though. He was as tough as nails. He loaded up his pack with ammunition. I couldn't even pick it up but he just lifted it and swung it on his back and he was up and away. He was a real tough fella.

They closed off the top of the station after the war. In 1946 they went out to muster one particular block. In those days they would tent out. The weather turned and they all decided to abandon camp and make it back to the shelter of the homestead. When they returned a few days later they discovered they had lost nearly all the sheep in the snow. It was a

National Dog Trials, Omarama.

A Makarora house.

The high-country life can make you a little shy sometimes. It tangles you up in your own little world and you can stop feeling part of anything else but what is out under the sky.

significant loss to the station and after that they didn't feel there was much use risking stock like that again.

I still think the autumn musters were the best time of the year. We would go away for a week, staying in station huts and would camp out if there wasn't a hut for the night. Now people move in and out to the muster on trucks so there is no need to stay away for the night.

I stayed at Algidus until 1964, getting married early the following year. We moved to a farm down the road, managing it for a while, before moving to a pretty isolated farm in the high country, near Tekapo, where we stayed for nine years. It was so isolated that it was too far for the kids to go to school. My wife schooled them from home by correspondence until they were Standard 4 (Year 6).

The last time I working up at Algidus Station, I was helping a friend who was its new owner. We mustered the whole place using a helicopter—just two of the dogs and us. I had mustered using helicopters before but nothing like the terrain of Algidus. You had to hunt up and down the spurs with the 'copter and we went in fairly close to the land. The helicopter was great as we zigzagged across the face of the countryside.

We carried the dogs with us in little dog boxes. I have to admit the dogs were more than a little resistant about getting into them the

first time we tried but they got used to them pretty quick. We would carry the dogs up, then I would come out at the top with the dogs to take the stock off the hill.

With the rougher bits we mobbed up the stock with the helicopter before I went down. We would do one block at a time and I would change the dogs after every block. They got tuckered out on the steep terrain.

Dogs are made for the big spaces. They love the work, they love to be kept busy with us but the autumn musters are hard on them. Walking on shingle is hard enough but running on it is harder still. The wind can blow it up, it rips into your skin and is rough on the dogs. Sometimes, after a full day of mustering, we would need to almost carry the dogs away in the morning—though once they spot the sheep they are away working again. The dogs are great friends. I miss it when I haven't got them. We are only on a quarter-acre section now and I have just the one pup.

I can't remember the name of every dog I have ever owned but each one has been important. I started off with only two. It is better that you focus on your technique when you first begin and make sure you work with just the two well. Being a good dog worker means you have to always find yourself in the right place at the right time. The dogs are only as good as the time and effort you put into them.

Grahame McKimpsky

CHRISTCHURCH, RABBIT CONTROLLER

Grahame is well known in the hills of the Canterbury high country with his distinctive caravan. Contracted to monitor rabbit numbers, he is a regular visitor to the stations and farms across the Canterbury region.

Near Lindis Pass.

MY JOB TAKES ME UP INTO THE HIGH COUNTRY all the time. I need to go out on to the stations and record rabbit sightings. We need to protect the pasture and keep the rabbit levels well controlled and at a manageable rate.

I have never actually lived up in the hills but since starting this job I often stay out overnight as it makes my job much easier to manage. I was managing a farm down south that went into receivership before I got this job. The farmer was selling off a pile of things before he left, and one of them was an old caravan He was only asking for $200 so I bought it and painted it up. It is fairly old and basic but it has everything I need. Now I just stay in that if I need to go up country for the night. I put in a generator so it truly has everything, and it is good to know I have a place to stay that I am familiar with.

The way I see it, if you are travelling around, by the time you do your day's work, eat something and then have a bit of a kip, it's time to start work all over again—it's easier just to stay out here. I don't go to a campsite or anything. Sometimes a station will let me stay on their land, but if they don't I just park up on the side of the road for the night. It is nice to have the flexibility really.

There is something quite amazing about the feel up here. I enjoy being outside just looking at the country views. I do a lot of walking for my job, and there is a real feeling of space that you don't get anywhere else. I take my dog Pat with me for company—it is nice to have someone to talk to.

I got the job after working with the regional council for a while helping with possum control. A lot of that work was closer to home and I didn't have long trips to get to the farms. After getting my current job, I didn't want to spend half my day out on the roads, so the caravan was a good option. I like the idea of rolling out of bed and being at work as soon as you open the caravan door.

I chose to do the rabbit work on top of the possum control just to add a bit of variety to my week. The job itself can be a little boring as it is a lot of sitting around, out walking just trying to find the signs, but you do get to meet some very interesting people and I enjoy that.

I didn't want to spend half my day out on the roads, so the caravan was a good option. I like the idea of rolling out of bed and being at work as soon as you open the caravan door.

Lake Lochnagar, near Mt Aspiring.

I am pretty good at cooking for myself while on the road. I do a lot of one-pot meals and I enjoy doing it all for myself. Once I get home my wife does a lot of the cooking but up here I get to be the one doing it all. I think she enjoys the nights I spend away too.

Wintertime can get pretty chilly up in the hills. There are nights in the caravan where it is too cold to peel off any layers and I just go to bed with all my clothes on just to stay warm. The best times of year are late spring and early autumn— special times of the year to come up here.

There are all sorts of ways you can tell if rabbits are about. Of course, there are always some around—they are never going to be fully eradicated. I need to look out for the telltale signs they leave like scratchings in the earth and droppings. There is a certain level that is acceptable for rabbit numbers but if you measure a higher level than that the farmers are then obliged to do something about it.

In the old days it was the council that paid to get rid of the rabbits. The farmers paid rates that covered all that sort of thing. Now, it is the farmer's job to cover the cost of rabbit control themselves, so they prefer the levels are maintained, of course.

When the Calicivirus was released a few years back into the rabbit population we saw a huge drop in numbers but in recent years the numbers have started to grow again, especially in North Canterbury and Central Otago.

I see quite a few hares around too. They can grow to a huge size and can be a little surprising if you scare one to running just in front of you as you walk. The hares are big eaters—they eat everything a sheep will. But they don't cause as much damage with their digging, not like rabbits do. A rabbit-hole can be rather treacherous to an unsuspecting walker or to stock.

You need to ask permission to come on to the property, which can be a little nerve-wracking if you don't know the person. But you do get to see a whole range of farms and farming styles. I have my own farm I run when I am not out rabbit monitoring and I enjoy looking at other people's farms and talking note of what is there.

Checking out the quality of the stock is always enjoyable. I think you can learn a lot

I see quite a few hares around too. They can grow to a huge size and can be a little surprising if you scare one to running just in front of you as you walk. The hares are big eaters—they eat everything a sheep will.

about the type of farmers there are by their stock. Some people seem to take a lot of effort over keeping the quality up while others just seem to let anything go.

I get just as much joy from seeing how the farmers set out their fences, the paddocks and tree lines. I'm really interested in gates and how farmers tie them—in fact I have been known to take photos of them. I could take photo upon photo of that. They don't just use proper latches—there is often a bit of twisted wire or some old string tying it shut. And they all have a special method to latching it back up quickly.

I am a born and bred rural man—I grew up on my mum and dad's dairy farm. When I got married, my wife and I worked on stations along the coast in the North Island. They were similar to the ones in North Canterbury as they were hilly terrain and remote. We worked with both cattle and sheep, and enjoyed it.

Later on we did 14 years on a deer farm. I was the day-to-day manager and we did everything from building races for the sorting, to creating a slaughterhouse on the property so we could export direct off the farm. It was the

sort of place that gets sold from one business to another rather than the type that is handed down from son to son. The owners don't tend to stick around but go where the money is. A lot of the stations I work on in the South Island now are still family ones, though it is starting to change here too.

I find the people out here good all round. Sometimes the regional council may have upset some of the farmers around here with a policy change or some such and being attached to the council means I am often the one who gets to hear about it. People can get a little grunty. But I see that as just part of the job. I don't like to upset them any more than they already are by not listening—they are already letting me on their land. Though if anyone declines, I am still allowed to come on as I have a warrant. It is just nicer to do it by asking first. Keeps everyone happy. No one has turned me down yet.

It can take a wee while to feel like they have warmed to you. People out here like to take some time to get to know you. They look carefully at you and make sure you are who you appear to be. Once they know you are straight up they are pretty friendly. Things just move a bit slower out here.

Ross Urquhart

North Canterbury, owner/lessee of
Flockhill Station

Ross grew up at Flockhill Station, leaving after it
was sold in the 1980s. Coming back to the station, as
an adult, was a return to a familiar home and place.

I WAS BORN IN DARFIELD IN 1957 AND GREW up at Flockhill Station. My father had bought it after the war and he moved the family there in 1949. He bought at just the right time as he hit the Korean wool boom in the 1950s and managed to pay off the whole farm within a few years, which made things quite a bit easier. It was not an insubstantial amount he paid for it either—but that wool boom really helped us out as a family.

When he first started on the station he worked it with just two other people. Things changed after it was paid off and we would have up to 10 regular workers with us helping run it. Things went full circle when I came back to run it with just two of us again keeping things ticking over. There is just not the money in it anymore to justify large numbers of workers.

When I was 17 my father died. It was the early '70s and my 19-year-old brother and I took it over and ran it. We ran it together for 10 years until the family decided to sell it. We both loved the place but could not afford to buy it ourselves.

I came to the North Island and farmed there for a while. The high country had got under my skin really and I had to come back. It was definitely a return due to nostalgia more than anything else.

It is hard to put your finger on exactly what makes the high country special. The mountain terrain keeps you fit, the sheer space is inspiring and there is a freedom you can't get anywhere else, especially when it's just you out there working against the elements.

The people are different too—a lot of fun and good to spend time with. They make you feel at home and there are a lot of laughs to be had. There is a diverse range of people and the community is close-knit. Most people get on pretty well and if there is ever something on they want to turn up and be involved.

We don't always have a lot of time left after we look after our own farms to help each other out. My poor shepherd one year during the summer season was exhausted by the time he got a day off. He was almost in tears by the time he told me. You get so busy and so focused you don't notice that the days are flying past without a break. The poor guy went for three months with only one half day off. We were working up to 90 hours a week. I had to give him some time off as soon as I realised.

There are hard times too though. It is not all just wandering around taking in the view. Dealing with foot rot and dagging sheep would have to be among my least favourite tasks. Foot rot seems to have only got worse over time. It never used to be so bad. It came onto the farms in the '70s and has stuck around ever since.

One of the most intense jobs would be growing and preparing winterfeed. The worst

They call dogs man's best friend and I can tell you it is because they get us to do all the horrible jobs for them! They might work hard for us but I am sure we work harder to make sure they are well looked after.

has to be killing dog tucker (killing sheep for dog food). They call dogs man's best friend and I can tell you it is because they get us to do all the horrible jobs for them! They might work hard for us but I am sure we work harder to make sure they are well looked after.

I have always had my own dogs, ever since I was nine. Even now, and I am not really on a farm, I still have a pup. He is the same bloodline of the dog I had at 17 years old. I normally have a team of about five or six but with only seven sheep that number would be a slight overkill at this stage.

I think mustering is the most fun—partly because it is social. Everyone enjoys a good muster. It is basically about showing the skill of your dogs—though, of course, dogs are just like kids in that they never perform when you want them to. They know when you just want them to show off and choose that precise moment to ignore your commands.

Besides mustering, the other time we got big groups of people in was when we had the shearers come in. My wife, Louise, still cooked for them and we would make sure they felt at home. It seems to be different in other parts of the country. My son went down south and said that the farmers and shepherds didn't communicate with the shearers but for us, when the shearers were on the farm we all worked together as a team. It was like having a gang of mates around working together.

Some of the shearers we had working with us were the same as the ones we had as kids. Some of them were managing to shear right into their 70s. One of the last gangs we had through— about eight guys—four of them were 65 or older. All blade shearers, all great characters.

I came back to Flockhill after 15 years. Someone else owned it then but I leased it. There is certainly a different feel to leasing as opposed to owning. You can't afford to invest in the land, as you know it is not a permanent thing. And it doesn't feel the same as owning a place for yourself.

After my father died we started a lodge that the new owners developed further. There had been the original homestead there but it had burnt down in 1969, the new home being built into the lodge. The new homestead is now part of the lodge.

The muster in March, with four mates from the North Island, would get 20,000 acres covered in four days. In the old days we would use horses and the same amount of space would take 14 days. The dogs would get tired and foot-sore and the days were a lot longer. With a Hilux we could throw the dogs on the back and cover that much more ground.

Horses might be nice to work with but in reality they waste a lot of time. Before we switched to using the Hilux we would need to start our day at 2 a.m., and wouldn't be getting back until 9 p.m. some nights. You would need

to get up, feed the horses, cook the breakfast, catch the horses and be ready for the day. You would start riding at 3 a.m. so you could be ready to start the muster at daybreak.

With a Hilux you get the luxury of a sleep-in to about 4 a.m., which is much more pleasant. I am glad for the improvements in machinery and technology too. We have bigger bales of hay made, which makes feeding out so much easier in winter.

I have never had a problem with vehicles in the snow, though I've had a couple of scares. Once, the tractor slipped in the snow a bit and went rolling down the hill with me in it. Once

it starts moving there is no real stopping it and you just have to wait until you grind to a halt. I have never got the ute stuck though, which must show a bit of skill because the stockman I had with me one year got stuck twice in one week. I guess you acquire a few skills just by using them all the time.

The high country is ever growing in popularity, particularly in the areas of recreation. There is a strong attraction to the hunting and skiing, and people in the area will probably continue to grow these sides of their activities to supplement their farming income.

There are more controls over what you can

Horses might be nice to work with but they waste a lot of time. We would need to start our day at 2 a.m., and wouldn't be getting back until 9 p.m. that night. With a Hilux you get the luxury of a sleep-in to about 4 a.m., which is much more pleasant.

and can't do, which can feel a little restrictive at times. The Resource Management Act and council regulations can sometimes make you feel like you are caught between what is officially permitted and what you feel is good for your land.

One of the biggest problems to the environment is the wilding pines, the self-sown pines that are spreading all over the high country. With some of the changes in grazing management, the trees are getting established where there have not been trees for years. The trees, broom and gorse effectively take over and the pasture is lost. I hope that one day we don't find that pine trees have taken over much of the high country.

I showed some people from the regional council the effects on my land at Flockhill. Where sheep used to graze down one of the gullies is now overgrown and taken over by self-seeded pines. Farmers can't afford to keep on top of it all, with everything else they need to focus on.

One of the main reasons some of the high country is reverting to exotic weeds is the removal of grazing animals. Closing the high country to prevent grazing will lead to an explosion of exotic pests and the destruction of tussock grasslands that we are familiar with today.

People are beginning to find new ways to make money off of their land. If you have huge amounts of capital, there is the potential to grow your farm and do well but many farmers as a rule don't have the kind of money needed to do that.

Moving into the recreational pursuits can be a positive option but it would be a shame to see some of the high country become closed up as farmers move out. These are areas that have been grazed for centuries— first by the moa and then by sheep. I can understand why people want to come out and enjoy the feel of the high country but I can, of course, understand why property owners want to fight allowing just anyone to come onto the land. I hope there is enough room for both recreational use and for farming to continue out there, that a decent balance can be found.

We have moved out of the high country, to a place north of Auckland. My wife is working in real estate and we have 30 acres. Our stock is going to total around 20 sheep and one dog. I would like to head back to the high country at some stage but in the end it is a matter of being able to go back. We will see.

Tommy Topp

WAIPARA, STOCKMAN AND FARM WORKER

Tommy grew up in the city, with a yen for farming.
Getting his first farming job at 15 gave him a taste
for the farming life, even if he wasn't allowed to take
it up. Later, he worked on Molesworth Station before
becoming a shearer and farm worker.

I DIDN'T GROW UP ON FARMS. MY DAD HAD worked on one during the depression but we grew up in the suburbs of Christchurch. I got a summer job at Balmoral homestead when I was 15 and loved it. The farmer there offered me a job and I took it.

I got back home and told my dad that I had a job and I was going to leave school. He wouldn't have a bar of it; said I had to finish school properly before getting myself a job. I was going to have to stay at school until I was 16 whether I wanted to or not.

The worst bit was ringing the farmer at Balmoral and telling him I couldn't come. He just laughed and said that boys did it to him all the time—accepting a job before being told by their parents they weren't allowed to take it up. I was just another one.

When I turned 16 I left school and went working on farms. I worked on a range of farms and was working on Molesworth Station when I hit 21. I thought I was going to get the day off for my birthday but was told I had to attend a calf market that day instead. As a treat I got to go the Top House for drinks and a bit of a party at the end of the day. There wasn't a pub close by at the time, though one did open up soon after.

I was a stockman at Molesworth. I worked with cattle on the flats. We had four other workers in my section with a head shepherd overseeing us and another man overseeing the stores and doing the books. We rode horses everyday, which I really enjoyed.

We got a fair amount of North Island workers down at Molesworth. I think they liked coming as it gave them a bit of a South Island experience. But farming is really the same anywhere. The main difference is you start earlier on a high country farm and you get to end your day a bit earlier I guess.

We lived in the single men's quarters with a cookhouse. The supplies would come in every Wednesday and we were looked after well. There was always plenty of tucker, whether they cooked for us or we were looking after ourselves. We would share the cooking between us men, depending on who got home first. It seemed to be pretty evenly distributed as we all got our fair share of cooking.

The worst bit was ringing the farmer at Balmoral and telling him I couldn't come. He just laughed and said that boys did it to him all the time—accepting a job before being told by their parents they weren't allowed to take it up. I was just another one.

Lake Pukaki.

I only worked at Molesworth for two seasons but really enjoyed myself. I was one of the first ones they paid for the whole year instead of just employing for a season. They started to do that because the workers would stop at the end, get a job somewhere else and never come back.

Back when I was working there it was so easy to find another job. If you didn't like where you were working you knew that there was always next door to take you—and they would probably offer you more money. I always felt that we were treated well though. The high country was known for treating its own well.

I think that is why we were taken good care of back then. They needed us more than we needed them. You got to pick and choose where and when you worked. A lot of the people don't bother to cook for you now. The young fellas used to be looked after by the boss's wife on the farms. She would keep an eye on them to make sure they were getting fed and tell them to phone home to their mums once a week. Nowadays, I don't think they care about those sorts of things too much.

I went shearing after I left Molesworth. Now, shearing is a year-round job but back then it was purely seasonal. You only got work over the Christmas period and then had to find other bits of work for the rest of the year. I did a whole range of farm work really—anything that kept me busy.

Back when I was working there it was so easy to find another job. If you didn't like where you were working you knew that there was always next door to take you—and they would probably offer you more money.

I managed to get one of the first railway houses put up for tender in Waipara. There were all sorts of government-owned houses up here—all of them are privately owned now, of course. It's a changing world.

Shearing was one of the better-paid jobs around. We would get £7 per 100 sheep and for a while there we had regular pay increases, good ones, every season. The pay made it worth waiting for each upcoming season and there was always plenty of casual work to add to it over the year.

I have spent my life working on farms or doing farm-related work. For a wee bit I did some truck driving, which was a nice change. For the most part, though, my life has been based around farm work.

I do a bit of work with a local guy and his Clydesdales. He uses them for the wine trails up here as well as for shows. Clydesdales are pretty versatile, though not so well suited for high country work. You're better to use a Clydesdale crossed with a thoroughbred. It helps keep their weight down and they tend to have a better nature too. The better the nature the easier they are to work with, which is important on the hills.

After I had been working and living in single men's quarters for a while I wanted a place for me and my future wife. I managed to get one of the first railway houses put up for tender in Waipara after I got married. It was a good buy back then. There were all sorts of government-owned houses up here—railway, power board and traffic board houses. Some of the wooden houses were moved to Twizel apparently, but the brick and permanent material houses stayed here. All of them are privately owned now, of course. It's a changing world.

Howard Birch

LEESTON, FREIGHT COMPANY OWNER

AND TRUCK DRIVER

Howard still works for the freight company he built
up, then sold several years ago. He knows every
weave and bend in the high country roads and has
met nearly every farmer from the Canterbury plains
to the West Coast in his time as a driver.

I THINK I KNOW THE ROADS UP THERE through the high country in Canterbury as good as anyone. I worked them for 15 years, going up to the West Coast every week through the Lewis Pass carting stock. Now I've sold the business I don't need to go out there but I do enjoy working for the new owners every now and again and taking the same old trips over.

My freight company was a family business. My grandfather started it in 1908 and I added a stock transport side when I took over. I sold it out five years ago when my wife got sick, and after she died a few years later I went back to work for the new owners again.

I enjoy the life of driving. I suppose it's in my blood and all that. We were always out in the trucks with my father and uncle doing furniture moving and general freight business. We would run a daily fright run from Christchurch to Leeston.

Being a truck driver was great as a dad—I used to take my girls over the high country with me. The trips were good for talking with each other and taking some time out together when so much of life was busy. I feel like getting to own my own freight company was a dream come true for a truck-loving boy. I never had any other ambition in life. Once you are in, it seems like the most natural job in the world to do. It is all about the adventure of new people and even though the road you travel is the same week after week, there is always something

new and different whether it be a new place to pick up a load, or a new contact at an old place.

My daughters were not interested in buying the business so we sold. I was the last of three generations. It was a major decision at the time but now I am pleased I made the break.

When I owned the business, I had five trucks just doing the Christchurch to Leeston work and I focused on driving over to the coast every week. I would be away every week for a few days. When I got home I would need to do all the bookwork.

These days, I work for the freight company as needed. I do all sorts of driving jobs for them. The other day I went up to a station to pour concrete for a new sheep yards. I took up a load of ready-mix concrete and helped out for the day. There are many things you need to know about each job. For this one, I need to mix up the concrete and know how to add in the right amount of additives for it go hard. You need to make it the right mix of shingle, sand, metal and cement. It is all written down of course, but the job is more than driving a truck around.

Now I just drive it is great to know I can simply walk away from the truck—I hated the bookwork. It never was something that came easily for me. There was so much you needed to check. We called the highway patrollers the God Squad—they always wanted to check our logbooks, seeing if we were overweight,

There has been the odd night the snow has come in or the weather has turned and you need to kip in the cab. Ice on the road can leave you in real trouble so you really need your wits about you.

checking how our brakes worked. Not being in charge of sorting that out is a relief.

There has been the odd night the snow has come in or the weather has turned and you need to kip in the cab. A wee bit of ice on the road can leave you in real trouble so you really need your wits about you. The key is to make sure the truck is full. I have carried a lot of cattle and sheep over the years but the odd load of deer has travelled in the back too. If I have nothing else to take I will carry a load of wood in the stock truck.

Part of the job is to load up the stock. You need to pen them up and make sure they get on the stock trucks safely. I used to have a sheep dog help me out to get the stock in. We had a great little dogbox on the side of the truck. The dog liked being down there—we used to have a little grating there so he couldn't get his head out. I noticed that a lot of the trucks now let the dogs stick their heads out. It can give you a bit of a fright to go past a truck and see this little head sticking out at the side. Some of those dogs can pull their heads out a fair way.

It takes about three quarters of an hour to load up the truck with a dog. The farmer helps a bit by making sure the stock is ready in the yards. There have been a few times when I'm loading up cattle and get a mad one or a bull that's a bit toey. Cattle tend to be a bit flighty; sheep are generally easier to deal with. A crazy cow can affect the whole bunch and you need

Grassmere Straight.

Most truck drivers will pull over if they notice a car is getting antsy behind them. Sometimes I feel like calling out to the drivers of those cars, 'You cranky buggers, do you want to live or die?

to make sure you keep a handle on their behaviour or you can get into a bit of bother.

You get pretty good at spotting the problem ones. You can see it in their eyes—they tend to hold their ears back a little, like they are pinned down. That is probably the easiest warning sign to spot.

I always loved the distance travelling but it could be hard on the body. Sometimes I arrived at 3 p.m. and would have to leave again at 6 p.m. If the rough weather hit I would need to sleep in the cab. I used to have a sleeper cab that I could curl up at the back and catch a few winks. A quick kip gives you a real energy boost. Otherwise, I would have some strong coffee or take a quick brisk walk outside to wake myself up a bit.

I have never had an accident in the truck but there have been a few close goes with cars. I bloody well don't want to ever have an accident. It would be very hard to get back into the truck after one. If someone were hurt, even if it was his or her fault, it would be hard to come to terms with it.

People tend to blame the trucks for accidents but there are a lot of cars out there doing some silly things around us and we find it hard to stop. Most truck drivers will pull over if they notice a car is getting antsy behind them. Sometimes I feel like calling out to the drivers of those cars, 'You cranky buggers, do you want to live or die?'

I used to really enjoy visiting people at the West Coast after I had driven through the high country. The people out there are very friendly and welcoming. I had a regular place to stay and they would always have the door unlocked with a meal ready in the microwave, a cold beer in the fridge. They were very trusting people. Salt of the earth types. Otherwise we would all stop off at pubs along the way—there are some good ones in the high country too.

When you've spent a lot of time out in the high country you build strong relationships with the regular clients. You look after them and they look after you. There is a sense that you are a family in some ways.

I have seen the high country change a lot over the years. A lot of the high country people I knew have sold or are selling up, and there doesn't seem to be those big holdings anymore. It is a pretty tough game to make a dollar from it and the sheep don't sell for too much these days. I've noticed a lot of overseas people buying properties up for their holiday homes, which is OK for them, but probably not good for farming.

It is strange when you go to a place where the place has changed hands. Some of them can be ruddy cantankerous but when you are in business you just need to grin and bear it. You can't tell them to stick it even if you want to. Luckily most of the people I have worked with have been top blokes, guys who are great to talk with and work alongside.

Lake Hawea.

Mike 'Bones' Evans

SPRINGFIELD, MUSTERER AND ENTREPRENEUR

Bones is a musterer, entrepreneur and, well,
a larrikin. Recently banned from the local pub he
used to own for disorderly behaviour, 'Bones' knows
how to live hard and play hard. He also knows how
to tell a great story.

Lake Tekapo.

I STARTED MY WORKING LIFE AS A FISHERMAN out of Kaikoura. Thought that might be a bit of fun but quickly changed my mind when during the very first week another boat lost a lad about the same age as me. I thought 'bugger this' and went inland to go mustering instead.

I was from a farming family and was the fifth generation born onto our farm. We had to sell it though, as my father got a crook ticker. (Probably from all the salt and dripping sandwiches he used to eat. Those were a favourite food of the old musterers and deerstalkers.) We then moved to Kaikoura. I remember he could have bought the whole Kaikoura Peninsula for £35,000 but he turned it down. Never quite forgiven him for that. It would be worth a fortune now!

I had dogs from a young age. In fact, the statue in Tekapo of the working dog , which is a tribute to the working sheep dogs of the Mackenzie Country, was modelled by the sculpturess on one of my father's working dogs. She modelled out of clay. It then had to go to England to get bronzed, which took a long time. It came back from England and the very next week the dog got run over by a car and a horse float. So all we had left was this lovely statue in Tekapo. But dogs have always been a big part of the family.

I went mustering up on a farm in the Kaikouras instead of fishing and wanted a dog. I asked my boss if I could have one and he said no, so I left and went to another station. For a while I was a bit of a lost soul wandering around. I turned my hand to everything really: from shearing to mustering to lambing beats. I eventually went a bit further south and did a bit of building for a while.

I went and applied for a job at Grassmere Station. There were two other fellas—the head shepherd and his mate. I drove up with a trailer load full of dogs on the back of my car. I had my interview then hopped back into the car to head back to Christchurch. I was about a third of the way back when I realised something was missing—there were no dogs at the back! The fellas had unhooked the trailer but wedged it in place so that I hadn't noticed. I had to drive all the way back, which they thought was hilarious. I got the job though.

Once I had started there was still a bit of ribbing going on. That always happened with the new blokes. I was out on the horses with them. One of them rode up beside me and grabbed the bridle out of my hands and yanked it off the horse's head. The other guy got out the stock whip and whacked the horse hard. Off the horse went with the two behind me on their horses cracking the whip. The horse came to a grinding halt at the gate, leaving me to fly over his head and onto the other side.

The new guy always got it. Soon after that, another young fella started and we were out killing lambs for dog tucker. We went first and killed our ones. I told him I would load up the gun and then gave it to him. He kept on taking

I got tennis elbow after some years and had to quit the sheep-dipping business. I thought I might like to buy a pub to run. I told a few fellas and one remarked, 'That's like leaving a rabbit in charge of lettuce!'

aim and shooting but the sheep would just sit there. We were laughing at him as he got more and more frustrated. Then we 'fessed up'—I had loaded blanks into the rifle so there was no way any sheep was going to die.

I went shearing for a bit because it was good money. The food was pretty basic. We seemed to eat a lot of watercress and pigs' hooves. The gang I worked with brought a cook in most of the time, though sometimes the station would provide one.

We had a cook at Grassmere too. He was as mad as a meat axe. He used to threaten us with the said meat axe if we walked into the dining quarters with muddy boots. Eventually we had had enough of him and went on strike. We said we would not eat from him anymore. The boss was scared enough of him to not interfere. Eventually he left, after not getting paid for a couple of weeks.

Working as a cook on a station was a lonely life. If you did get a good one you looked after them pretty well. We had a great one once—a young girl who was bloody marvellous. Even if the sausages were burnt or the roast dry we didn't care. She was cute. She was clever too. She ended up becoming a doctor later on.

After a few years I bought a wee bit of land and bought a sheep-dipping business that operated through central Canterbury. I bought a sheep conveyor belt that made the whole process a lot easier. The sheep walk onto it and then come off their feet and down they go. It's a bit like a factory.

I used it to do pretty much everything on farms all over the place. You can easily drench them, vaccinate, check their mouths and then ear-tag them. You get a bit of a line going and it speeds the whole process up. I used to be able to crutch them too (removing the wool away from the rear end and legs of a sheep), which was good. I got a ute and would attach this contraption to the back of it and we would be off. It was good for treating foot rot too, though trimming up the feet would leave us all covered in blood. You'd have to chomp the hoof off a bit then put the sheep through a foot trough. Doing that allows the chemicals to get into the feet and clean it up for good. That's the plan, anyway.

I got tennis elbow after some years and had to quit it. I couldn't lift a thing. Not even a beer, which was a tragedy. I thought I might like to buy a pub to run. I told a few fellas once at a dog trial and one remarked, 'That's like leaving a rabbit in charge of lettuce!'

After looking all over I found one on my doorstep—the Springfield Pub. I put in a real low offer and bought it. I ran it for three years and then an Aucklander came along about offered me shit loads for it. I thought it was a good time to get out.

It got a bit of press though. When the smoking ban came in I got in a big stock truck and converted it to a smoker's bar up on the top deck. You could sit on the top there and it was just beautiful. With 80 per cent of my drinkers being smokers I needed to do something for them.

Speed shearing champs at Springfield Hall.

I have also had a bit of fun as a poet. The poems were pretty rugged, pulling the piss out of high country musterers. A mate of mine, Clifton Ashwell, and I made up a live show called 'Outside Bob'. Then we got a few others like Big Jim Morris and Ross MacLeod to join us. Jim only lasted a couple of shows before his missus pulled him out. She thought it was a bit disgusting. Then me and 'Mac' (as Ross is commonly known) did our maths and worked out the money was a lot better if it was divided by two instead of four. We went out on the road performing. Our show lasted about five years, going down a treat with the crowds, especially with the sheilas.

We did a few rugby clubs and it was a pile of fun. Then we made up a little book called *Bad Language*. I sent it to Whitcoulls and asked if they would sell it. I never heard back so I gave them a call. They said they loved it but didn't have shelves high enough. I offered to wrap it in cellophane for them but they said it was beyond that even.

I have also done a touch of inventing. It all started with a machine that made skinning rams easier. I am not a big lad—hence the nickname 'Bones'—and I needed something that made a heavy job easier. We manufactured and sold a few but they were a bit big and too hard to ship.

The most successful invention was the Bonefide Gudgeon Guide. It is designed so you can hang the gate on the guides, test swing it, then drill the holes for the gudgeons (the things you screw into the posts). It won an invention award at Fieldays and sold them at fairs. A stock firm in Auckland ended up buying me out, which was great—got to love those Aucklanders! (As long as they don't beat us in the Super 14.)

I then created Bonefide Crop Cutter. It was to help put electric fences in crop fields. You attached it to the front of your bike and it cut a thin trail only the width of the bike so you can then easily put in the fence. That sold quite well too.

I get bored easily I guess, and like the idea of developing something new. I guess I like to have those little diversions. It makes a change from other aspects of high country life. The hard bit is the marketing. I can't be bothered with that.

The high country can be incredibly isolated. It is so easy to find your own space and area on your own. Working dogs in such challenging country is a thrill. You always have your hard days but when the sun is shining it is beautiful.

It's not so pleasant when it's snowing. You leave the sheep on the hills as long as you can before the snow comes, which means if you don't time it right you can get caught out in it during the muster. If you get a big enough snow you can get stuck in the huts for three or four days. Last year we got a big snow mid April. There was an initial snow, that then froze, then another snow on top of it made the muster a bit treacherous. You generally want to get those sheep down to the flats to eat their tucker in the winter.

With most high country stations, most of the land is mountainous. The flats need to be saved

Now we have motorbikes and helicopters to help with the mustering. We used to scoff at them in the young days. Now I just enjoy the lift.

for winter feed, so the sheep are sent up the hills after shearing in early spring. They lamb up in the foothills then move their way further up during the summer.

I now own six acres in the middle of Springfield and lease another 1000. I still do a bit of mustering on top. Farming always pulls me back though. I think it is the dogs. I have had a passion for working dogs since I was young and it has never gone. Here on my wee block I have three sheep and five dogs. Those poor sheep are a bit outnumbered!

I am training some dogs up at the moment. I am running a huntaway at the trials. It gets into your blood and you meet up with other people in the high country that you don't see any other time. It is like a big reunion, a good social time.

I have just started mustering again too. I had to give up smoking so I can get fit again and I recently got barred from my own pub for being a bit disruptive one night, so that is helping with the drinking a bit. (All I did was wake up some backpackers.) They've banned their best customer.

Mustering can be really isolated work. At some of the stations I worked, you would be out of the way for a month, going out for a beer, say once a month, then heading back into the hills. You would stay in the single men's quarters and, while you would go out in the morning together, once you are on the hills you split up and are on your own.

Now we have motorbikes and helicopters to help with the mustering. A few stick to the old

ways but I'm getting old now so I never mind the helicopters. We used to scoff at them in the young days. Now I just enjoy the lift.

Another benefit of helicopters is you get to see where the sheep are. The pilot drops you up high and you can get started a lot earlier, while the day is not too hot. You drive the sheep down, sometimes into a central basin. First task is to round up all the sheep that have managed to wander off again.

I did enjoy riding out on horses but you needed to make sure you looked after them. If the horse went lame you needed to get off and walk. You learnt how to shoe your own horses pretty quickly.

Most of the time musters have been all-male exercises but we had a woman mustering with us the other day. Women are great out there because they can make so much noise they hardly need dogs. They can clear acres with their screaming. Most of the women I have seen out here are the daughters of station owners. Some of them get involved in the dog trials and are pretty smart cookies.

You don't need to be born and bred country to succeed out here. On of my best mates came straight out of town and has ended up one of the top huntaway men. Just goes to show you can come from anywhere.

I am still developing ideas linked to my passion for the high country and often go back into stations like Castle Hill and Mt White. I now own a store and café in Springfield so I guess that is probably where I'll hang me boots up!

Mt Aspiring.

John Higgins

SPRINGFIELD, SHEARER, MUSTERER, FARMER

From shearer to manager to musterer, John has
experienced most aspects of high country life in his
70-plus years. Though most of his days are currently
spent caring for his wife, the pull of the hills takes
him out to work on a nearby station every week,
allowing him time to reconnect with the landscape
he is so familiar with.

Merinos in front of the Craigieburn Range.

I HAVE KICKED AROUND THE HIGH COUNTRY for most of my life, except for seven years I spent travelling around shearing and transport driving. I grew up in the hills in Kaikoura, on our family farm. I was bred on steep hill country so farming on the hills is in my blood.

I was put to work when I was five. Before school I would have to bring the cows in for milking ready for my parents. They milked 40 cows every morning by hand. It was my job to get them ready.

I got my first dog when I was nine. He was a great wee pup. The boss from the farm my father was managing thought so too, and offered me £15 for him. That was a lot of money in those days so everyone was pretty surprised when I turned him down. My brother was impressed at my dedication to this pup and could plainly see he was a special dog. He asked me to come and stay with his family for a while as he helped me train the pup up.

That holiday ended up being a good six weeks away from school. I had a great time, though I later heard the school was trying to track me down. They were not too pleased at my casual attitude to school. I did miss a fair bit of it back then.

That pup was a good working dog and started me on my love of training dogs. After him, I became quite a lover of dogs.

My father was a strict man, a hard task-master. By the time I was 12, I was helping with the shearing, expected to blade-shear 100 sheep a day. It is not what I would have called an eight-hour day—it was more like nine hours, sometimes more. As I admitted earlier, I wasn't a regular at school either. Work on the farm would often keep me close to home, helping out where needed. It was also due to where our farm was situated. It was often cut off in bad weather when the river was in flood and getting to school often proved impossible.

I knew I wanted to stay in the high country. I had mates who were mustering so that's what I took to when I had to make my own way. It was a decision of what felt most natural and it was a good fit with me. I later went shearing, when I was around the 30-year-old mark. It wasn't blade-shearing like when I was a boy; by then we had machine shearing.

My father was a strict man, a hard taskmaster. By the time I was 12, I was helping with the shearing, expected to blade-shear 100 sheep a day. It is not what I would have called an eight-hour day—it was more like nine hours, sometimes more.

Farming has become a lot more sophisticated than it was in my early days. There is far more bookwork and you have to be as much a bookkeeper and a businessman as you do a farmer.

I used to travel around from place to place. We never went more than we could in a single day for the shearing. I was newly married so I wanted to come home each night.

Shearing did not captivate me like farming did. Farming was in my blood. I had that short stint mustering and then the run shearing and had to go back to working on farms. I ended up managing a hill property out in Springfield.

I managed several properties before that. Some were high country and the others were flat. I always preferred being out on the hills though. After a while, the jobs ended for one reason or another, such as the place selling up or owners dying. We eventually moved into Springfield and bought one of the old railway houses. They are all privately owned now. We got it for a great price—it's no doubt worth a lot more now.

In between jobs I would take on casual work for a neighbour, on a farm of approximately 7000 acres. Even now, I will go and work at the hill property out at Springfield. I still enjoy climbing the hills and work out there several times a week.

The combination of the open air, the wide spaces and outstanding views, together with the nice people you meet out on the visits create truly fun times. You may work hard but you also have a lot of fun attached to the job.

We start the day out in vehicles that take us up to our starting point. We walk from where

they drop us, which vary from day to day. It's usually done in a series of day trips now—unless you are mustering on some of the very big stations. In days gone by we would have been mustering away from home for a fortnight, camping out.

Farming has become a lot more sophisticated than it was in my early days of farming. There is far more bookwork and you have to be as much a bookkeeper and a businessman as you do a farmer. There's far more cleared country than we were ever used to as well, as the technology is there to clear the steeper terrain much better than we ever could.

Shearing life has changed since I was doing it. It was once normal for all the food to be cooked for us. That doesn't happen anymore. Mind you, it at least means you have a better idea of what you will eat, given you bring your own. I remember being at one station where the wife of the farmer came in to tell us our lunch was waiting for us in the shed and that she was off to town. At lunch time we went in to eat and discovered we each had one jacket potato wrapped in a lettuce leaf. That was pretty grim. Of course, we just ate up—there was nothing else much you could do.

Most of the places had basic fare and there were a few places that put a real effort into it and you looked forward to eating there. Springfield was known to be a place where

Torlesse Range at sunset.

farmers did not provide for both the shearers and workers overly well. A lot of women didn't know what sort of difference it could have made to us to take us out a cold drink or a bite to eat.

I emphasised to my wife that if you look after the shearers then everything is easier, that you get more of out of the workers. And she became quite renowned for her good cooking. People still comment on it today.

In the end, though, I was never overly concerned if the women didn't supply us meals. But most of the women were very good to me. Some would open their homes and invite me and other workers to eat with the family, which was always appreciated.

In the last few years my wife's health has failed and I have moved into a new role. I had to learn how to cook for the first time at the age of 72, which was a bit of a shock to the system, but I think I have the hang of it now. It has also meant I had to cut back on my outside work as I need to be close to home to care for her. I feel that she cared for me for the first 50 years of our life together and this is my chance to give back to her.

I have found the reduction in my outdoor time pretty hard. I feel best when I am outside in the open air but I'm slowly adjusting to the change. I still need to get out and around. If I sat down for too long I might pack up. I may be

I feel best when I am outside in the open air—I need to get out and around. If I sat down for too long I might pack up. I may be a skinny fella but I am very fit. I try to take a day or so at least every week out there helping on any of the local farms.

a skinny fella but I am very fit. Being able to walk the hills and getting out amongst others is a big thing for me so I try to take a day or so at least every week out there helping on any of the local farms.

Being out in a rural community is still working for us, though that's partly because I am still able to drive. There is no public transport service out here—not anymore. It used to be that you could catch the train into Christchurch late afternoon, do your shopping and catch the train back again in time for tea. Now you really need to be able to drive. If I didn't have my licence I would be in the cart, as I like to put it.

Even though I am not working so much on farms anymore, I still have my dogs. I have always had at least three working with me, though four is probably ideal. I've just bought a new pup for $300. It is the most I have ever paid for a dog in my life but I have had a bit of a bad run with the heading dogs I've got recently so thought it might be a good idea to invest in a pup with a good working pedigree. If I am out on a muster I might borrow another dog, probably a header. But I usually have enough of my own to sort it.

A heading dog is used to head off the sheep during a muster. They are quiet dogs, whereas huntaways are bred and raised for their loud barking. You need their noise to be heard by the sheep so they go where you want them to. They are your voice out there on the hills. They chase the sheep whereas the heading dog will stand and stare the sheep away.

Then there is the handy dog. They are a mix between a huntaway and a header dog. They can bark but not as loud as a huntaway—but they know when to stay quiet too.

I used to get into the dog trials but not so much these days, as I'm not able to get decent practice time in to warrant it. But good work is done at those trials; it's there that huntaways really come into their own. If they can cut through the noise at trials they can do it anywhere.

I think I'll never get tired of being outside in the high country. Not only is there great people out here who are good company but the whole atmosphere is wonderful. Sometimes you are out on a hill and you look out and you can see for miles. The sky is blue and the air is still and it is just you and this huge expanse of beauty. It doesn't matter that it is isolated. It's just beautiful.

Henry Barker

QUEENSTOWN, STATION OWNER AND MUSTERER

Coming to the high country in his late teens,
Henry Barker missed learning the finer details of
running a high country station. He and his brother
quickly adapted however, owning and running Ben
Lomond Station near Queenstown. Even though Henry
now lives in Queenstown, he can still be found helping
out on the odd muster or tramping in the local hills.

The road between Lindis
Pass and Wanaka.

I WAS 18 WHEN I FIRST MOVED TO THE HIGH country. My father bought Ben Lomond Station with the plan that my brother and I would be able to take it over when we were old enough. His family had a farm in Balclutha but he found it far too wet and cold and wanted a place that was drier and a bit warmer.

The farmers got the hard land in the high country. The miners had come in and taken the easy bits for their mining (the gold, of course, was located at the foot of the hills and close to the rivers). Our station was a hard place to farm with a lot of mountainous areas and difficult terrain. Looking back, the climate has definitely changed as well.

In my day there was more snow. It would be cold enough to be able to skate on the pond in Queenstown. The winters were hard and cold, and snow would last for at least six weeks. The summers were hot, making up for the bitter cold. Now the winters are milder and the summers are cooler. There are less of the extremes that we experienced.

We had good access to the homestead. It was only four kilometres to the main road. When we needed to bring in fencing materials they needed to be dropped in from a fixed-wing plane so for that we used pack horses. Later on, of course, there were helicopters for that sort of task.

The homestead was between Queenstown and Arrowtown. It is a busy stretch of road now but back then you would have been lucky to get two or three cars on it in a day. No one much minded having a sheep or two across their path.

Our woolshed was down by the roadside too. That all had to change as the popularity of Queenstown grew and the road began to hold places of interest that caused people to drive along it. There was a pub and many other attractions. And people did not really enjoy having to manoeuvre their cars around the sheep.

My brother Maurice and I took over when I was 23 and he was 26. We owned it together for 23 years. We would have about four or five men out with us to do the shearing every year as well, so there were always people on the station for one reason or another.

The farmers got the hard land in the high country. The miners had come in and taken the easy bits for their mining Our station was a hard place to farm with a lot of mountainous areas and difficult terrain.

In winter the tracks around the station would become frozen so we used to need to walk everywhere—it was far too treacherous to take the horse out in that weather.

Isolation was never a problem as the station is really quite close to Queenstown. If I wanted a bit of extra company I could just drive down to the pub or into town.

With farming in the high country, you just turn the stock out and then let them alone. There is no feeding them throughout the year, though you might have put aside a few bales of hay for the rams and cows in the winter.

Once the snows came you needed to get out and check the stock. If a sheep got stuck in the snow, the keas could come and kill it. We would need to go out and make sure we knew where the sheep were and check they were all safe.

Winter made the homestead a cold place. It would be surrounded by snow during the winter, though that is rather rare now. The tracks around the station would become frozen so we used to need to walk everywhere—it was far too treacherous to take the horse out in that weather.

A few years after we took over the station we went out to check stock after a heavy snow. There had been one fall of snow, then a freeze and then another heavy snowfall over that. The snow could fall hard.

There was once an avalanche too—to this day we don't know what triggered it. I was standing at its edge and got caught up in it. The snow was incredibly heavy and tossed me down, swept me up and sent me down the hill. I got thrown against a rock, which while it hurt, ended up helping me get moved from the main thrust of the avalanche.

Luckily, my brother was there to help me once everything calmed down. It took me a long time to get over it though. I was always very cautious in the snow for about two years after it and had ongoing problems, worrying that it might happen again. I am still unsure how it got me.

We had never expected avalanches I guess. Our father never really taught us of the dangers of high country farming before we took over and we were all surprised such a thing could happen. We made some effort to stop such a thing happening again by installing a snow fence across the snowline, to prevent the sheep going too high up the mountain.

After several years, my brother went and worked on the mission field in New Guinea so I had to run the sheep station by myself. My parents had moved into Queenstown by this stage, after having stayed with us for a few years first.

I got in a few housekeepers while he was away and I used a lot of casual help for the big jobs around the station. Before he left we spent quite a bit of time putting in a lot of fencing. That significantly cut down the mains power needed on the station for mustering. We would need at least two men to help on top of any neighbourly hand.

Having neighbours help each other out was an essential part of surviving. It cut down labour costs significantly and we would all chip in and

Mt Aspiring.

help each other during the busy times. We got to know each others' land and were familiar with it all.

Soon after he got back from New Guinea, Maurice got married. For a few years we all farmed together on the station. We decided to sell after thinking it might be a good idea for us to both have our own farm. Neither of us had had a family that would be old enough or able to carry on and as the country was hard, it was not a place you could run into your old age.

Looking back we perhaps did not sell at the best time for both of us. Wool prices were at an all time low when we sold and then, just as we were each getting ready to buy a new farm,

the economy changed again and prices all went up for land. Maurice had bought a farm but I went and worked at the meatworks in Dunedin for a while

I found it was a lifestyle that really suited me. I could work for eight months of the year there, then go and help my brother for a bit on his farm—and still have time to enjoy my passion of tramping and exploring.

Walking the hills was always something that came natural to me. At 74, I am not as quick as I once was (I used to be the fastest man on the hills). Though only last year I went out and helped the new owner at Ben Lomond muster.

Walking the hills was always something that came natural to me. At 74, I am not as quick as I once was (I used to be the fastest man on the hills). Though only last year I went out and helped the new owner during the Ben Lomond muster.

It wasn't until my brother owned his farm that we realised how easy life in the high country was. While there were a lot of hills that needed climbing, it was less work than a lowland farm. We used to think we were hard done by because we had to get up early in the morning and chase the sheep in the steep mountain country. We had no idea. If we went out mustering and it started to rain, we would just stay in the hut for the day. But on a lowland farm you have to go out in the rain. You need to work no matter what the weather.

Farming has changed over the years. I think we had it pretty easy. I can see how hard they work now and the days are a lot longer. There seems to be a lot more work and the pace is faster, which is interesting because they also have more mechanical and technological help.

I remember when we were going out for the muster, we would ride out to the huts and take a pack horse with all of our supplies. We would ride out to the sheds and huts but from there on in it was all done by foot, as the land was too steep for the horses. They were there really just to help lighten the load when transporting our supplies. We used the horses to help check the land too. We had a track around the perimeter of the station that we took the horses around.

During lambing weekend, for instance, people would come onto our land to shoot goats without our permission. The loud bangs would scare the lambs and cause the ewe and lamb to become separated. We would need to keep a close eye on them.

The end of the day was the end of the day in those times. The people working out at Ben Lomond now can work up to 10-hour days. We seem to have had a lot of down time in those huts in my day. We had plenty of relaxed times, finishing at about 3 p.m.

Now with the use of helicopters, you get the sheep in early then go and get another lot. The day seems to go on for a long time. The workers nowadays will often have to work in the yards after a day's muster as it takes less time to muster owing to modern transport.

In my day it wasn't a bad life. I had good company, interesting things to do and wonderful hills to tramp on. We may have thought we had it rugged but really it was a good life, an enjoyable one.

A hut near Kawarau Gorge.

Barry Drummond

Cass, railwayman and 'mayor of Barrytown'

Barry came to Cass in Canterbury for three years
and stayed for 20. Nearing retirement, he has
watched the changes in rail use through the high
country. Barry lives in the last house owned by the
New Zealand Railways Corporation for
employee use in New Zealand.

Lake Pearson.

THEY CALL ME THE MAYOR OF BARRYTOWN because I am the only fella who lives here. I actually live at Cass at the railway station. Someone gave me a sign they had pinched from the real Barrytown, so the locals renamed this little area after me.

I came to Cass 20 years ago to work on the railroad and am still here. Most of the time my days are all about track work, making sure the track is all clean and tidy and in working order so that the trains can pass by safely. In winter there is a lot of going out for emergency mends with the cold weather making the passing a little dangerous at times.

Most of the trains are coal trains, taking the coal across from the West Coast to Christchurch. We get the TranzAlpine scenic train in every day but that never breaks down. The freight trains carrying milk powder come past too. It is mainly the coal and freight trains that break down and I need to make sure the track remains clear and problem-free when they do.

When the weather turns bad you know the tracks might be affected. We had floods one year and the track got washed out. Luckily, we found the areas before the trains came past so we stopped any accidents from occurring.

The big snow of 1992 was huge. It hit us big time and took a lot of managing. For some reason we were not so badly hit by the snow of 2006 and it was reasonably easy to clear it.

I have worked in railway all my life. I started in Mosgiel, working there for a few years. They asked me to move around a bit, which is how it was all done. You expected to move if you worked for the railways. I was asked to go to Otira for two years and then come here for three. I said that was fine but that it was pretty remote and so I wouldn't be happy to stay for more than that. When I got here, though, I felt like I fit right in and here I am: 20 years in the same place.

I am still sort of surprised at myself that I am still here. The people in the community have been so nice to get to know and the time seems to fly so fast. The years seem to link up with each other and just run away on you. I am quite close to Grassmere Station and I get on really well with the people up there.

Being the last person to live here can sometimes feel a little odd. When I first arrived,

When I got here I felt like I fit right in and here I am: 20 years in the same place. I am still sort of surprised at myself that I am still here. The years seem to link up with each other and just run away on you.

Early morning, Cass Station

there were another 12 to 15 people in the town. Now there is just me. The railway jobs that used to be here all the time are now contracted out from the ministry works base in Springfield.

Otira was once a busy railway town too and now there are only about four people living there. The railway community has got a lot smaller over the years so you get to know them all pretty well. All the drivers and workers know each other and keep up with what is happening.

There are some other buildings out here, besides my little house. My house is the last house owned by the railways for staff use. There are four other houses here too. A doctor lives in one and the other three are holiday homes. The university owns a big building out here too, that they use for courses. They have a field station for some of their papers so we get students out here sometimes.

I started the Cass Bash a few years back and it seems to get bigger and busier every year. It started when I found a keg of beer to share with the locals at Christmas time. It has got big enough for people all around to come and have a bit of a party. I run it on the last weekend of November and it is a huge celebration. The whole community is invited as well as all the other railway workers around the area. People come in from Auckland, Palmerston North and Invercargill—anyone connected with the railway and their families are included, so that's a lot of people.

Otira was once a busy railway town too and now there are only about four people living there. The railway community has got a lot smaller over the years so you get to know them all pretty well.

Barry's backyard—Mt Misery.

I wouldn't consider myself to be railway mad or anything. I am not the sort to go rushing out as they go past, counting carriages or noting any differences.

We put on a game of cricket. It is always the railway workers against the locals and it is a lot of fun. We have a railway social club that comes up in the first week of December with a kid's party so the end of the year can be pretty festive.

The social side of being up here is good. At Christmas time there can be up to 15 people here and we all have a good laugh together. There is always something on and something to do.

I have seen a few changes to the types of trains in usage since starting here. We had old electric trains then diesels. There is less emphasis on passenger trains, and freight is really for coal and dairy more than anything else.

The trains are my job but I wouldn't consider myself to be railway mad or anything. I am not the sort to go rushing out as they go past, counting carriages or noting any differences. Some people run out and take lots of pictures but that's not really my thing.

I guess I stand out a little in these parts because I don't work on a farm. There are not many of us who aren't farmers around here. We have a few who work for the Department of Conservation but that is about it as far as variety goes.

I have never been a train driver—never had any desire to be one. I can stop a train if I have to in an emergency but that's all. I need to have a job that keeps me moving. I would find the sitting down all day too difficult. I need to be doing something.

My normal working day starts at 7.30 a.m. and goes on to four in the afternoon. Being by myself, though, I can get called out at any hour of the day. The other night I had only just got into bed when the call came that there had been a breakdown and I had to go and help them offload. But that doesn't happen every day. Sometimes, if it happens in the dead of the night, I can wait until morning, which is better.

I guess one of the best bits of being here by myself is that I can sleep in a bit if I need to on those days where I have been up half the night before. I might not get up until half eleven, and then it isn't too long before knock-off rolls past again.

While the numbers of railway workers has really dropped since I first started in the railways, there will always be someone out here. It is too isolated to run from another area. I can't see myself here of another 10 years—I plan to retire in another five. But it has been nice to be able to stay in one place for so long and put down some roots.

I am not too sure if I will stay out here when I leave the railways. It probably isn't the best place to live out your retirement years. I think I will find a nice spot where I can mow lawns or something. Something to keep me active and busy. That would see me right.

Alf Phillips

Coalgate, shearer

Starting shearing from a young age, Alf quickly saw
the benefit; though the work was back-breaking it
was very well paid compared to many other jobs back
then. Alf has seen the changes in shearing from the
gangs to the contract workers, through his many
years in the high country.

WHEN I FIRST STARTED SHEARING, LIFE was pretty good. I was one of the youngest around. I had wanted to shear because the money was a lot better in shearing than in anything else that was on offer. Most jobs paid about 10s a day; for shearing you earned 36s per 100 sheep. At the beginning I struggled to make that number in a day but soon I was able to hit a target of about 140 a day. The pay worked out to be significantly more than any other job.

I started shearing at 16. It was a social business and there was a lot of travel involved. I worked all over the Hororata and Lake Coleridge regions. It was a big adventure for a youngun. There were no contractors or middle men in those days. We arranged everything and would move from farm to farm, staying in the shearer's quarters. I enjoyed the fact that at the end of a hard day you could just go back to the quarters and rest up in preparation for the next day.

The first three weeks of shearing nearly killed me. I would look at all the guys who were working and wonder how they survived. I used to have to lie down on my back for bouts during the day until it eased enough to keep going. I didn't care where I lay my head as long as I was getting a bit of a rest. After the three weeks it eased a bit and I came right. My body must have got used

to it. I never had back trouble after that, for which I was grateful, as back problems can be a common issue for many shearers.

The shearing was physical but in some ways was easier than now. The sheep have got a lot bigger than they were in my day. I guess they were not so well fed back then and the farmers have concentrated on breeding them bigger for more meat over the years.

The farmers' wives would feed us. They would make sure we were never hungry, and make us feel at home in our quarters. We would go in for regular meal times during the day. You needed to eat a lot and frequently to keep your energy levels up.

When it began to change and we were just expected to come out for day visits then go back again, it was not so appealing. Adding travel on to a hard day of shearing always felt a bit much.

We would work in teams of twos or threes, depending on the size of the farm. Some of the very big stations might have a team of up to eight, which was a large number to put up during the job. The number of shearers really depended on the size of the shearing shed. If the shed was bigger, we could send in more shearers. The farmers and any of their farm workers would pitch in too, which also influenced how many of us would come onto the property.

105

When I first started working on farms it was still very much the horse era—not many tractors were to be found. That has all changed now, of course, and people will choose tractors and other machinery over animals unless the terrain won't permit it.

Now, the shearers work at any time throughout the year but on those days it was very seasonal. We would get work from October to the middle of February then have the rest of the year off. During the time off I worked as a labourer on farms. I did everything and anything. I used to enjoy riding the horse teams and tractors

I moved out of shearing when I was 28, 12 years after I had started. I preferred the older methods. Farmers were starting to use contractors and it all became a lot more impersonal.

In 1955 I bought my own farm and still work on it now. It is a sheep and cattle farm primarily, though I have done a wee bit of cropping as well. It was a shift coming from a job where I was visiting other people's farms to a position where we had to get others in to help us.

I never had contract shearers in, though I have had people help here over the years. When we started and the stock numbers were lower I did the shearing all myself but the farm grew to a point where I had to get others to help. I had a farm worker with me

for a good 30 years, which was good.

Most of my place is leased off now by my daughter. I still like to be outside and involved but it is too much to run by yourself at this stage of life. Farming has changed over the years. It is not nearly so labour intensive as it was and tasks such as harvesting have sped up with specialised contractors coming in and the technological developments in farm equipment. But it is still very much so a physical job—you need to be able to be prepared to work the long hours when you need to.

I think one of the best things I did was to learn to shear. It paid off long term for me. When we bought the farm there were some seasons when I needed to prop up the income a bit here and there. Being able to shear was a valuable skill. Once the place was up and running I didn't need to do it anymore. .

The employment scene has changed a lot. It was a good life for many single men who would work from farm to farm, sometimes staying on the same one for years. Now contractors do much of the same work. Instead of employing an extra labour unit on your place it makes sense to just get someone in for the job you need, as you go.

A big part of my farming life has been my dogs. I have had them all my life and started dog trials when I was 13 years old. They have

A glimpse of Lake Coleridge.

All I ever wanted to do was farm. I have never had a desire to live in the city. I decided early on that the city life and me would not mix. I have been out here nearly all my life and could never go back.

always been working dogs rather than pets. I still participate in the trials and work with my dogs. I have four: two heading dogs, a huntaway and a handy.

I believe in training them myself. Some people don't, they prefer to get someone else to do it. It is something you either like or you don't. I quite like dogs and training them is all part of owning them for me. Some others prefer to purchase a dog already trained but for me I need to start with them right from the beginning.

Just like racehorses, you can have good and bad dogs. You want an intelligent dog and some are more intelligent than others. You want a dog that not only can do what you tell it but also be clever enough to be able to do it without you saying a word. A dog like this is easy to work with. They know the hows and wheres and whens, and they just get the job done.

The breeding does make a difference. A dog with a good pedigree stands a chance at being a good dog. Dogs that have been bred from a line of great workers are going to start to display those characteristics. What was a lucky dog becomes a dog that has

replicated its best bits in its pups. I have bred some of my own dogs, which has been good, as then I know what I am trying to produce. Otherwise I just go for word of mouth and pick up dogs from people I know.

If I thought my dogs were great, I can see that the benefits of breeding good dogs is shown in an overall improvement in the types of dogs at trials. The standard is still the same but there are just more dogs performing at a high level. Some of these younguns have a real way with dogs.

It is good to see the next generation continuing with the things that were part of our love for the life out here. All I ever wanted to do was farm. I have never had a desire to live in the city. I decided early on that the city life and me would not mix. I have been out here nearly all my life and could never go back. I have always needed to spend the bulk of my life outdoors.

I think it is the open spaces out here. I know it can be quiet almost anywhere but out here, with the space between you and the sky, it is a different sort of quiet. It fills you up with it all.

Charlie Draper

KIMBERLEY, CONTRACTOR, FARMER AND PILOT

Returning to the country he loved as a child,
Charlie built up a successful contracting business,
which he used to purchase his dream farm several
years ago. He worked through many endless nights
preparing the stock feed for the following harsh
high country winters.

Baling under the Torlesse Range.

I FIRST CAME TO THE HIGH COUNTRY AS A small boy. We came as a family but when I was 11 my dad was killed in a car accident and Mum couldn't support us out here. Three years after he died, we left the farm and moved into town.

Life changed direction after that. I loved the country and always felt a pull to it but living in town meant I went in a 'town' direction. After leaving school I became a fitter and turner and worked around Christchurch.

I married Jo in 1980 and we started our family of four children, beginning with Richard and Rebecca, who were born in Hornby. After five years of living in the suburbs, it was time to move back to the country. We were fortunate enough to be able to buy a 60-acre block in Sheffield. Later on we had our third and fourth children, Michael and Tim. We bought a 60-acre block in Sheffield and I began years of commuting in and out of Christchurch to my job there.

All that travel was fairly exhausting, so I took the chance for redundancy and the paying out of my super when it came up. With the help of a business partner, Barney Lloyd, I bought part of Taege and Holliday, building the business up.

When Barney died three years later, I took over the business completely.

We baled to all sizes and shapes—big squares, medium and rounds. Two years after we began we also started to produce silage and soon after that we moved into baleage, which is wrapped silage. That led ourselves to expand again into excavating and loader projects as we already had the equipment there for the silage and baleage side.

Cows eat anything but silage gives them the best feeding value for protein and everything else. The thing is, creating silage is a bit of an art—it needs to be safe to eat. It is made by carrying away the hay as soon as it is cut without letting it dry out at all.

Baleage is a mix between silage and hay, and is safer. but hay takes a week to dry. If the rains come before then, you run the risk of the important nutrients being washed away before it dries. Baleage only takes a day or so after cutting to make, so there is less of an issue. It smells a lot sweeter than silage.

We do the odd bit of hay but it's not as common now. It is a riskier option for farmers as it can be easily ruined if it rains.

I loved the country and always felt a pull to it but living in town meant I went in a 'town' direction. After leaving school I became a fitter and turner and worked around Christchurch.

I have always worked up in the backcountry, around Rakaia Gorge and Mt Algidus. The backcountry people are people I have come to know and consider friends.

A lot of my business involved carting and selling the baleage to other farmers. I sometimes felt I was a bit like a food bank. I would end up selling extra supply to locals and to farmers on the coast. Some people would want to sell their extra stores and I always had some of my own to sell on as well.

We would come in and do the whole thing for farmers. We would supply the rakes, give them plenty of options for wrapping and cartage, and do as much or as little as the farmers wanted us to do. Every farmer had a different level of participation and we would just work in with whatever they wanted to do.

The business just grew and grew—almost more than I had ever expected it to. It grew into a large operation and kept me very busy.

I have always worked up in the backcountry, around Rakaia Gorge and Mt Algidus. The back-country people are people I have come to know and consider friends. They have always looked after me and the boys I have with me on a job.

I have a very good client base. I feel like my clients are the best in the country. You feel like there is a level of mutual trust—you know they are not trying to shaft you and you would never shaft them.

The business required a lot of night-time work, with very long hours in the summer months. It was hard on the family, with us working a lot of hours when everyone else was socialising and out at barbeques and other summer parties. But to be

a successful contractor you need to be able to live it and eat it.

In the end the business just began to feel a bit too big for me and I sold off the silage side of the business to another agricultural contractor. I downsized the winter work so I could concentrate on the baleage, the hay and the straw.

While the business was building, Jo and I had plans for our own farm. Four years ago we tendered for a farm in the same district I had had to leave all those years ago. We won the tender and moved in. I sold the rest of the business last year to have more time to commit to the property.

I still have a fair bit to do with the buying and selling of product and work in an advisory role for both the new owner and the farmers. I still make my own baleage in summer, fatten lambs and graze dairy cows.

I look back at what we've achieved and feel like we really got somewhere. With both of us coming from a farming background it has been good to build a strong rural business. Now we have sold it, it's good to be able to take a step back and start to enjoy what we built up. It took a lot out of us for years and now it is good to just enjoy the rewards of our labour.

I actually think it nearly grew out of hand. Bigger is not always ideal and sometimes it ruled my life. During the summer, I would often work 100 hours a week—working hard, with a lot of physical work.

I still don't sleep well in summer. You try to survive on four hours of sleep at least but often you would get less. You dread anyone who rings you right at the end of the season, as you are just so very tired. Those jobs are the hardest ones to do. But in the end you just do it.

As part of rural living we have involved ourselves in the community. It is part of your job really, part of what is expected if you are going to involve yourself in a rural business. I have done a range of things, from being on the school board of trustees, the volunteer fire brigade and the Lions Foundation. It does mean going to a lot of meetings but these turn into social events as well and you foster great networks.

The kids went to local country schools and got a different type of education from mine. Country schools have all these little extra benefits that city schools miss out on. Richard is now a genetic scientist, Rebecca is a kindergarten teacher and the other two are still at university and school.

All of the boys have worked in the business, which has helped them fund their education. They all started at the bottom and worked their way up, learning on the job.

Finding good employees is always important—you want people who are going to last the distance. It is very much seasonal work, starting in October and ending in March. I ran a good base of seasonal workers and tried always to employ locals, though we would need a top-up of overseas staff to fill the gaps. I have employed a lot of clients' kids for a season or two. The work fits in with university and school holidays rather well.

A few years back I picked up a boy who was too young to leave school but finding it hard to

You need to have some passions in life and flying is one of mine. I have a strip at home so really it is about as easy as it is to jump in a car. It is one of those things I need to do and has made all the hard work worth it in the end.

get into it. He worked with me for a day. I told him when he had finished his schooling I would give him a job. Two years later his dad rang and said he was still keen. He is now engaged to my daughter so it just goes to show you have to be careful who you employ! I have been very lucky to have some amazing staff around me in my work. I am well aware that staff can make or break a business, and the people around me have always worked hard and done well.

Needless to say, you need a very understanding wife and family to run this type of business. They miss out on a lot. They miss out on the normal family times many other families take for granted. We even used to work Christmas day every year, which was hard on the kids.

One year I did a job for a guy at Christmas and he never paid me. I realised that working on Christmas day was just not worth it so from that year we changed it so that everyone gets the day off. The guys get New Year's off too—from 8 p.m. to midday the next day. You need to give them the morning off to give them time to sober up, as they need their wits about them on the job.

Contractors tend to come and go on farms and generally farmers don't give meals. We have found, however, that we have been well looked after by high country farmers. They know we have often already worked long hours before we get there and that we'll be much more effective if we can get a bit of a feed and keep the fluids up. Getting fed is definitely a bonus

when working on the backcountry farms.

We worked the low country farms on the flat, too. We would start on those in October and move higher up country as the season progressed.

The business allowed me to involve myself with another passion of mine—flying. I have been flying since the 1970s. It's a good way to check out the properties of neighbouring farmers. It is also a way to get to some of the more remote areas, to check on clients. Using the plane, instead of driving, saves a considerable amount of time: I have a lot of clients on the coast I need to visit, and the plane is great also for going to clearing sales or to check out some lambs.

All of this, of course, is just my official excuse for getting in the plane. You need to have some passions in life and flying is one of mine. I have a strip at home so really it is about as easy as it is to jump in a car. To be honest, even if I couldn't think of an excuse I would still fly. It is one of those things I need to do. It has been one of the things that made all the hard work worth it in the end.

I look back on the times we had when the business was so busy and feel I came away with a lot: the good people I have met, the friends I have made—well, you can't take any of that away from me. I feel my memories of working backcountry, and the people I have worked with, has added a richness to my life I couldn't have got anywhere else.

Snow Cleaver

PORTERS PASS, STATION MANAGER AND MUSTERER

Born in Northland, Snow decided to come to the
high country with a mate. Fulfilling his promise,
he came for a few years and never found a good
reason to leave. The pull of the hills continues to pull
stronger than anything else. Give him a horse, some
boots and a couple of dogs, a hill to work on and
Snow is happy.

I HAVE BEEN CALLED SNOW FOR YEARS.

I was so named by my uncle who had been in a prisoner-of-war camp with a man called by the same name. I reminded him of that man and it sort of stuck.

I have worked in the high country and in the remote parts of the South Island for most of my life. I was born in Kaitaia and had a great mate there who I had planned to come down south with. We were about 14 at the time and had both seen a programme about mustering in the high country. We decided we would come down here and try our hand at it the moment we turned 15 and could leave school.

My parents brought me up on a dairy farm. I had well and truly had enough of dairy cows by that stage and had no intention of sitting around all day milking cows. I wanted to be active and move around a bit.

Six months before we were due to go my mate got crook. He had leukaemia and died a short time later. I wanted to complete what we had agreed to do so I threw a couple of dogs together, put them on the train and came down.

The original plan was to come for a few years and then go back home. But I kept on doing casual mustering—there was something to it that I really loved. I moved around different stations a bit and saw some beautiful bits of the country. The stars are an awfully long way above you and the sheep on the hills are so calming. The spaces are amazing, the air so clean and the river waters blue.

I worked in town for a while to find a wife. It backfired on me. I was working at a sawmill during the day, which was fairly mindless. It was noisy and dusty and you worked to the clock rather than to your natural rhythm. I would come home and stare at the hills in the distance. You could see them above the smog and they looked much more peaceful than the noise of the mill.

One night I just had to get back to the hills. I threw a swag together and grabbed a couple of dogs and left for the hills. I haven't really been back to the city since. I headed down south and went mustering from station to station for 20 years. I worked in a few places for a good while, as the station manager at Mount Hyde, for instance.

I moved around different stations a bit and saw some beautiful bits of the country. The stars are an awfully long way above you and the sheep on the hills are so calming. The spaces are amazing, the air so clean and the river waters blue.

I developed things down there and it was going really well by the time I had finished.

When I first came to Castle Hill I would sit up on the verandah and worry I had come to a place that was too busy. The house is a lot closer to the road than I am used to and I could hear the traffic go past. Within a month I had sort of got used to the busyness but it was still a lingering concern. I thought I was going to have to leave and go back to somewhere quieter.

I have been at here for 18 months now and have only gone over the pass to Christchurch twice in that time. I get the old girl to go in for supplies. As long as she comes back with my bankcard and the supplies I am happy to stay

out here. I notice when I go to Christchurch that it feels very crowded. There are so many people around there you feel like they are all breathing on you. I can never wait to get back to my open spaces.

There is always someone popping in home to say hello. When all is said and done though, I enjoy the company of my horse and my dogs. It is good thinking power time. When I go into town the pressure of business drowns out any ability to think. People out here live longer because they can hear their own thoughts. It is about strong bodies and strong minds.

I prefer Canterbury high country to anywhere else. Up here you can look at the sky and it is as blue as can be for as far as the eye

I arrived here in the early 1970s—a lot of farmers were still using packhorses and hacks for mustering. I loved working with the horses and still do. We still use horses a lot at Castle Hill—I prefer animals to machines any day.

can see. Down south you look up and there's usually some sort of cloud in the sky. We get these lovely warm days here in summer but even in the heights of summer down there, you can still feel a chill in the air behind the sun's warmth. We get cold weather here, of course, but it is a dry and beautiful cold.

I arrived here in the early 1970s. It was the last days of farmers using the high-tops. A lot of farmers were still using packhorses and hacks for mustering. I loved working with the horses and still do. We still use horses a lot at Castle Hill—I prefer animals to machines any day. I know a lot of people have reverted to choppers and vehicles but I don't find horses are any bloody slower than a vehicle.

To be honest I haven't got time for vehicles at all. It only takes a split second with a machine to have an accident you will regret. Horses are different: much more reliable and they are with you all the time. You don't need to think about where you put your keys or walk back to where you parked the bike. If a spark plug packs it in you have to walk back with the bike. Horses are much better to work with.

I have been working with horses for 20 years. I worked on a place out the back of Oamaru that I completely broke in with horses. I've work with Clydesdales a bit too, though we don't use on them on the farm. You would be surprised to hear how many people still use them, particularly in smaller places down south. I think with the fuel crisis going the way it is, using animals is a good plan. Lower cost and less stressful.

My dogs are important too, of course. I do the dog trials and always have them with me on a muster. I went to a dog sale the other day with Bones, who is an old mate of mine. We have known each other for 35 years. The dog sale was disappointing in itself but the trip back was good—we didn't get round to returning home until the next day. You've got to play a bit every now and again.

Farming is all about listening and watching the cycles. I've noticed people are beginning to go back to some of the old ways, perhaps because they work and fit better with the world the way it is.

I start my day during the winter around 7.30 a.m. You are very much run by whether

When my time comes all I want to do is go out for a walk and find a quiet spot, a lovely, peaceful spot for my resting place. This is my home and I feel very settled here.

the sun is up or not—any earlier is too dark for work. We can easily work seven days a week in the busy times. Castle Hill has gone under a huge amount of development with a lot of over-sowing and fencing being done, which can require long hours.

Both are excellent ways to build stock. It is a struggle to make feed in this type of country, as the growing season is so short. You have to constantly be thinking of how best to manage the feed and the stock. You need to feed the land before you take from it so the investment in the pasture and fencing is well worth the effort.

Farming has gone though some tough times, basically since the 1980s. The thought back then was that the strong farmers would buy out the weak ones, leaving super farms that were strong and viable. But the government underestimated the power of the farmers' ties to their land; the sense of battling through—so many farmers have just sat here struggling and sticking with their land.

The high country is a bloody great spot to be. It is a safe and lovely place to make your home. I notice more and more townies come into the area, particularly Aucklanders. The Department of Conservation has opened up a lot of areas around here and people want to make a connection with the land.

I can completely understand that. It is why I want to live out here, after all. We get the clean air and natural exercise of walking the hills. Even when you go mustering you are moving downhill with the sheep. All you need to do is stick on a pair of hobnailed boots and away you go.

I struggle with the way they treat the land more than anything else. It isn't the extra people but the rubbish they leave behind. We have these beautiful paddocks, so pristine, suddenly littered with chip packet wrappers and plastic bottles. The visitors seem to have little respect for the environment and see our home, our business as their playground.

The more the area's advertised and the more people that come here just increases the danger to visitors' safety. Visitors can have no idea of just how fast the weather can change up here, especially between March and September. It can be very easy to find yourself caught out without appropriate clothing and no way to get home. Last winter was fantastic as we had about two feet of snow for quite some time, which kept all the visitors away. It was very peaceful.

I think the high country is where I'm meant to be—it's the best place to live and a good place to die. When my time comes all I want to do is go out for a walk and find a quiet spot, a lovely, peaceful spot for my resting place. This is my home and I feel very settled here. As long as my legs can cart me around, as long as I can get on a horse, I am here to stay. Here's to the high country.

On the drive to Wanaka.

Acknowledgements

John Bougen captured each man so well, and shared his viewpoint of some of the most beautiful scenery in the world.

Thank you to Geoff Walker for his shared love of the people, the landscapes and the light of New Zealand's high country, and to Jeremy Sherlock for being such a great editor to work with.

It was an honour to speak with each man in this book, and thank you also to the wives and families for sharing your mountain men with us.

Glenys, you were a great mother hen to share any new developments with. As usual, thanks need to go to my children, who were ever-patient when told that yes, Mummy was working on the book one more night.